FOLKTALE

by Natalie M. Rosinsky

Compass Point Books ✦ Minneapolis, Minnesota

Compass Point Books
3109 West 50th Street, #115
Minneapolis, MN 55410

This book was manufactured with paper containing
at least 10 percent post-consumer waste.

Managing Editor: Catherine Neitge
Page Production: Bobbie Nuytten and Ashlee Schulz
Photo Researcher: Svetlana Zhurkin
Library Consultant: Kathleen Baxter

Creative Director: Keith Griffin
Editorial Director: Nick Healy

Compass Point Books would like to acknowledge the contributions of Tish Farrell, who
authored earlier Write Your Own books and whose supporting text is reused in part herein.

Library of Congress Cataloging-in-Publication Data
Rosinsky, Natalie M. (Natalie Myra)
  Write your own folktale / by Natalie M. Rosinsky.
      p. cm. — (Write your own)
  Includes index.
  ISBN 978-0-7565-3516-2 (library binding)
  1. Authorship—Juvenile literature. 2. Tales—Juvenile literature. I. Title. II. Series.
  PN3377.5.T35R67 2008
  808'.066398—dc22   2007033094

Visit Compass Point Books on the Internet at *www.compasspointbooks.com*
or e-mail your request to *custserv@compasspointbooks.com*

About the Author
Natalie M. Rosinsky is the award-winning author of
more than 100 works for young readers. She earned
graduate degrees from the University of Wisconsin-
Madison and has been a high school teacher and
college professor as well as a corporate trainer. Natalie,
who reads and writes in Mankato, Minnesota, says,
"My love of reading led me to write. I take pleasure in
framing ideas, crafting words, detailing other lives and
places. I am delighted to share these joys with young
authors in the Write Your Own series of books."

Share Wit and Wisdom

Are you ready for talking beasts and wise fools? How about clever mischief-makers and magical events? These are part of folktales told around the world. Long before stories were written down, storytellers spoke, sang, and chanted these tales to delight listeners and teach children good behavior. Most folktales are simple enough for children to understand yet complex enough to satisfy adults. Many tales are funny, while some are spooky or sad. Whether they cause laughter or tears, all folktales communicate a people's values, even religious values still practiced today.

You can share such wit and wisdom as you write your own folktale. This book contains brainstorming and training activities that will help you sharpen your writing skills. Tips and advice from famous writers and examples from their work will help you create storytelling magic. Your imagination will be your bridge into the worldwide tradition of folktales.

CONTENTS

WANT TO BE A WRITER?

This book is the perfect place to start. It aims to give you the tools to write your own folktales. Learn how to craft believable portraits of people and other creatures. Plan perfect plots with satisfying beginnings, middles, and endings. Examples from famous books appear throughout, with tips and techniques from published authors to help you on your way.

Get the writing habit

Do timed and regular practice. Real writers learn to write even when they don't particularly feel like it.

Create a folktale-writing zone.

Keep a journal.

Carry a notebook—record interesting events and note how people behave and speak.

Generate ideas

Find a folktale you want to tell or retell. Who are its characters, and what are their problems?

Brainstorm to find out everything about your chosen folktale.

Research settings, events, people, and creatures related to the folktale.

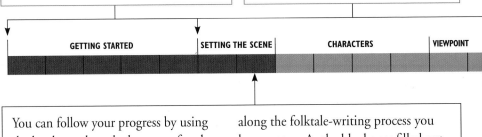

| GETTING STARTED | SETTING THE SCENE | CHARACTERS | VIEWPOINT |

You can follow your progress by using the bar located on the bottom of each page. The orange color tells you how far along the folktale-writing process you have gotten. As the blocks are filled out, your folktale will be growing.

Plan

What is your folktale about?

What happens?

Plan beginning, middle, and end.

Write a synopsis or create storyboards.

Write

Write the first draft, then put it aside for a while.

Check spelling and dialogue —does it flow?

Remove unnecessary words.

Does the folktale have a good title and satisfying ending?

Avoid clichés that do not suit your goals.

Publish

Write or print the final draft.

Always keep a copy for yourself.

Send your folktale to children's magazines, Internet writing sites, competitions, or school magazines.

| SYNOPSES AND PLOTS | WINNING WORDS | SCINTILLATING SPEECH | HINTS AND TIPS | THE NEXT STEP |

When you get to the end of the bar, your book is ready to go! You are an author! You now need to decide what to do with your book and what your next project should be. Perhaps it will be a sequel to this folktale, or maybe something completely different.

YOUR CREATIVE LIFESTYLE

What tales have already been told about creatures whose adventures demonstrate human vices and virtues? Are there more stories about tricky characters who outwit themselves as well as others? Which parts of the world have tales about whole towns filled with fools? Find out by doing research in the library or on the Internet.

When you start to write your tales, you will need handy tools and a safe, comfortable place for your work. A computer can make writing quicker, but it is not essential. Your imagination can work wonders even with simple tools.

What you need

These materials will help you organize your ideas and your findings:

- small notebook that you carry everywhere
- paper for writing activities
- pencils or pens with different colored ink
- index cards for recording facts
- files or folders to keep your gathered information organized and safe
- dictionary, thesaurus, and encyclopedia

Find your writing place

Think about where you as a writer feel most comfortable and creative. Perhaps a spot in your bedroom works best for you. Possibly a corner in the public library is better. If your writing place is outside your home, store your writing materials in a take-along bag or backpack.

Create a folktale-writing zone

- Play some of your favorite music or music of the people whose folktales you have read.
- Use earplugs if you write best when it is quiet.
- Decorate your space with pictures of folktale characters or of places associated with folktales.
- Place objects that hold good memories from your own life around your space.

Follow the writer's golden rule

Once you have chosen your writing space, go there regularly and often. It is all right to do other kinds of writing there—such as a diary or letters—as long as you *keep on writing!*

CASE STUDIES

Rafe Martin uses a computer to write in his home office. He writes each morning, sometimes stopping to walk around the room while he reads his work aloud. It is important to this storyteller to hear how his tales sound. After lunch, Martin writes more, answers mail, and reads.

Adèle Geras used to write lying down on a sofa. She enjoyed writing in what she describes as "beautiful hard-backed note-books." When she wrote her first long novel, she tried writing with a computer. She now uses a computer for all her writing. Geras writes every day when she is at work on a novel, aiming for 1,500 words at a time.

GET THE WRITING HABIT

Before you can write fantastic folktales, you have to build up your writing "muscles." Just as an athlete lifts weights or a musician practices scales, you must train regularly. You cannot wait until you are in the mood or feel especially inspired.

Now it's your turn

Discover other folks!
Increase your knowledge of famous folktales. Look at a collection of ancient folktales such as *Buddha Stories*, retold by modern writer Demi. Read the *Adventures of Brer Rabbit*. Try a collection such as *Favorite Folktales From Around the World* to discover tales from a different continent. Find and read at least three tales that you have not heard of before.

In your writing place, use pen and paper to brainstorm about these folktales. What do they have in common? What do you like most or least about them? Your answers may provide you with the elements for your own folktale!

Tips and techniques
Set a regular amount of time and a schedule for your writing. It could be 10 minutes every morning before breakfast or one hour twice a week after supper. Then stick to your schedule.

Now it's your turn

Explore a folktale favorite

Around the world, folktales offer different explanations for how creatures came to be as they are. Read a collection such as *Native American Animal Stories* to learn how one culture explains "Why Coyote Has Yellow Eyes." Look at Rudyard Kipling's famous *Just So Stories* for his ideas about creatures around the world.

What animals, birds, or insects are native to your area? What creatures are you familiar with as pets or pests? Does your family or community already have its own stories about these creatures? Perhaps the inspiration for your own folktale is as close as your next-door neighbor! Take 10 minutes to brainstorm.

Jot down details about creatures you have known, seen, or heard. Do not worry about grammar or spelling—just let the ideas flow freely, like water from a pitcher on a hot summer day. You are on your way to being a writer of folktales!

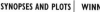

KEEP TRADITION ALIVE

Some writers of folktales retell stories from their own tradition. Adèle Geras does this in *My Grandmother's Stories: A Collection of Jewish Folk Tales*. Laurence Yep draws upon his Chinese background for his folktale collection *The Rainbow People*.

Native American writer Joseph Bruchac tells tales from his own Abenaki tradition. He also travels each year to gather the stories of other native peoples from their own elders. Bruchac values these firsthand experiences. He says, "I hold the memories of those stories and those places, and I know that they will give me a certain balance when the time comes for me to write about any of those things."

Virginia Hamilton and Julius Lester retell stories rooted in their African-American heritage. Yet a storyteller need not belong to a tradition to tell or retell its wonderful tales. Verna Aardema wrote African folktales, but she was not African or African-American.

Tips and techniques
Ask an adult for the correct ways to thank elders or storytellers for sharing their people's tales and wisdom with you. Other people's customs may be different from your own.

Now it's your turn

Listen to your own folks!

What tales are part of your own tradition? Ask your relatives and neighbors to share stories with you. Listen and gather ideas from answers to questions like these:

- What bedtime tales did *their* parents and grandparents tell them?
- What stories were told at family gatherings?
- Do they associate certain stories with having good or bad luck?
- Is there one character or group of characters who appear in many tales?
- Are there tales told about special places or historical events—such as droughts or wars?

Now brainstorm ways you could add to the traditions of your own family. Spend 10 minutes jotting down ideas, thinking about "what happened next" or "what happened before" the tales you heard. This sequel or prequel might be the folktale you write! If this exercise leaves you smiling, you are on the right path as a storyteller.

CASE STUDY

Joseph Bruchac puts a new twist on an old saying about teaching children. The cautionary words to "Spare the rod and spoil the child" aren't used. Instead, he writes that "throughout Native North America the rule was 'Spare the rod and tell the story.'"

Tips and techniques

Use a tape recorder or take notes while you gather folktales from relatives and neighbors. Not everyone is comfortable being tape-recorded, so be certain to ask about this at the beginning of the interview.

FIND YOUR VOICE

Being a good reader is the "magic ingredient" in becoming a good writer. Reading will help you develop your writer's voice— a style of writing that is all your own.

Finding your writer's voice

Writers continue to develop their voices throughout their lives. Skilled writers also learn to change their voices to match their subjects. When you read as a writer, you notice the range and rhythm of various authors' words and sentences. Rudyard Kipling's humorous style uses a rhythm that echoes the dialect of English once spoken in India. Kipling also playfully uses grand words and long formal sentences. Rafe Martin and Nina Jaffe describe places and events in great detail. Learning to recognize how various writers craft their stories is like learning to identify different types of music.

Writers' voices

Look at the words and sentences these writers use. Which writers use short as well as long sentences? Do you think this choice works well? Which writer has a character talking? Was this an effective choice? Which writers use many detailed descriptions? Which writer uses words that rhyme? How does that choice make this writer's voice stand out?

And what was this? Wherever those tears fell, the flames went out! Glistening tears dripped from burned branches and soaked into scorched earth. The forest became quiet and still. Then, wherever those tears touched, new life burst forth! Green grass pushed up from among still-glowing embers. Blossoms opened. Leaves unfurled.
Rafe Martin, *The Brave Little Parrot*

In the sea, once upon a time, O my Best Beloved, there was a Whale, and he ate fishes. He ate the starfish and the garfish, and the crab and the dab, and the plaice and the dace, and the skate and his mate, and the mackereel and the pickereel, and the really truly twirly-whirly eel. All the fishes he could find in all the sea he ate with his mouth—so!
Rudyard Kipling, "How the Whale Got His Throat," in *Just So Stories*

Hungbu waited patiently, and when he saw that the gourds were ripe and ready, he and his wife and children went to the garden to harvest them. He reached out to pick the first gourd. Before he could touch it, it opened up all by itself, revealing inside—not pumpkin flesh and seeds—but yards and yards of shimmering silk and handfuls of shining golden coins. Hungbu and his family stared in wonder.
Nina Jaffe, *Older Brother, Younger Brother: A Korean Folktale*

| SYNOPSES AND PLOTS | WINNING WORDS | SCINTILLATING SPEECH | HINTS AND TIPS | THE NEXT STEP |

GET YOUR FACTS STRAIGHT

Often folktales are set in the past. They may also be set in a faraway place. If you are writing about unfamiliar things, use the library or Internet to get your facts straight. If your tale is set in India, what animals are native to its jungles? Which kinds of fish or other creatures swim in its rivers?

CASE STUDY

Virginia Hamilton said she discovered many folktales in "old manuscripts or out-of-print materials that are languishing in libraries." She used university libraries near her Ohio home, state folklore societies, and collections of stories gathered in the 1930s by the U.S. government. In her books, Hamilton—like Nina Jaffe—always explains where she first heard or read a tale and who told it.

Now it's your turn

Head outdoors

Many folktales have scenes set outdoors—in forests, on mountains, or near the ocean. Visit the nearest natural spot with your writer's notebook. Look around. Close your eyes and breathe deeply. Listen carefully. Run your hand through the grass, along a tree trunk, or underneath a snowdrift. Now take 10 minutes to jot down all the details you discovered. Use these details to help readers experience your folktale world.

Learn your lesson!

Folktales often teach a lesson about what a particular people consider good or bad behavior. Have *you* recently been praised for a good deed or scolded for a bad one? Perhaps it was your brother, sister, cousin, or friend who "learned a lesson" this way.

Find and retell a folktale that describes similar good or bad behavior. Or write an original folktale of your own that "teaches" the consequences of such behavior. Spend 15 minutes in your writing place brainstorming ideas. Will you have human characters, or do you have other creatures in mind to represent you, your friends, and relatives? Have fun thinking about what sorts of creatures those might be! Demi's *Buddha Stories* or Rudyard Kipling's *Just So Stories* might provide some inspiration here.

Tips and techniques

Virginia Hamilton urged writers to "carry a notebook with you at all times. That way you'll never miss an important moment."

CASE STUDY

Some folktales around the world are chanted or sung to the beat of drums. For her book *Patakin: World Tales of Drums and Drummers*, Nina Jaffe continued the practice of drumming she had begun in college. She researched and included in *Patakin* information about the kind of drum accompanying each tale. Jaffe also describes what this drum music sounds like and includes musical notes for trained musicians.

A WORLD OF WONDERS

In your folktales, you reveal a world full of wonders to readers. Your setting will seem sharper, brighter, and clearer through the many details you describe. Readers will feel as though they are right there—even without a storyteller's drum really beating nearby!

Sensational nature

Your attention to detail and your imagination will also help you create scenes of magical places. Use as many of the five senses as you can to bring a scene to life. Adèle Geras does this in her retelling of a Jewish folktale about a selfish wealthy man named Bavsi. He has never cared about hungry, poor people. A wise king invites Bavsi to dinner to teach him a lesson:

> *After the soup came a whole fish baked in vine leaves and laid on a bed of rice. Then came roasted meats. Then cakes dripping with honey and studded with nuts, and velvety fruits fragrant with luscious juices, and with each course the same thing happened: the food was taken away from Bavsi before he had time to touch it. Bavsi felt completely bewildered.*
> Adèle Geras, "Bavsi's Feast," in *My Grandmother's Stories: A Collection of Jewish Folk Tales*

Readers can almost smell, feel, touch, and taste this tempting meal! We understand how this experience finally makes hungry Bavsi more sensitive to other people's hunger.

CASE STUDY

Adèle Geras used her own grandmother's apartment in Jerusalem for the setting of her collection of Jewish folktales. She admits, though, that she did not hear these tales from her talkative grandmother. Geras learned Jewish folktales from other people and through research.

In her retelling of a popular Korean folktale, Nina Jaffe adds sight, touch, and sound to her "sensational" description of a bitter journey one family takes:

> *And that very afternoon, he and his wife and three children set off down the mountainside, with nothing but a few belongings on their backs, to find a new home. They walked for miles, up and down the steep hillsides and rocky paths. The wind blew in their faces, and the dry leaves crackled under their weary feet.*
> Nina Jaffe, *Older Brother, Younger Brother: A Korean Folktale*

Readers can feel the wind and hear the leaves as well as see that rocky path.

As real as life

In this tale about the African mischief-maker Anansi, Verna Aardema uses many real-life details about where and how the Ashanti people live. She tells how they make fish traps from certain trees, what kinds of reeds grow in the river, and which creatures live there:

> *Anansi and Bonsu went looking for material for the trap. They found some raffia palms. And Bonsu said, "Anansi, give me the knife. I'll cut the branches. And your part will be to get tired for me."*
> *… By weaving and tying, weaving and tying, he finally finished the trap.*
> *… Anansi carried the trap into a patch of water reeds near the shore. As he was tying it to a reed stem near the bottom of the river, his groping hand disturbed a crayfish.*
> *Then kapp! A huge claw clamped down on to his little finger.*
> *Waaaaaa! Yelled Anansi, as he came splashing out of the water—the crayfish dangling from his hand like a fish at the end of a fish pole.*
> Verna Aardema, *Anansi Finds a Fool: An Ashanti Tale*

These details could come from firsthand visits to Africa or—as was true of Aardema—from research about people and countries there.

CREATE IMPOSSIBLE SETTINGS

Folktales sometimes include settings and actions that are impossible in the real world.

In his collection *Mysterious Tales of Japan,* Rafe Martin tells of a fisherman named Urashima Taro who was brought to a magical kingdom beneath the sea. Martin uses specific details and real-life comparisons to make this impossible situation seem more real to readers:

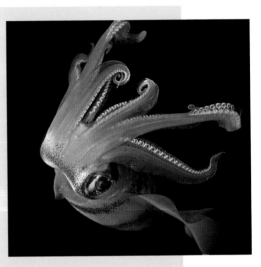

Every day some new wonder was brought to entertain him. Sometimes it would be a pearl, but a pearl bigger than any ever seen, a pearl as big as a man's head. And the light shining from that pearl would be so bright that it could illumine a whole chamber of the palace. Sometimes giant sea serpents would coil around the stairwells of the palace. Then the light shining from their bodies would make it seem as if the stars had come down from the night sky. Sometimes an octopus or a squid would follow behind him the way a dog or cat might follow a person.
Rafe Martin, "Urashima Taro," in *Mysterious Tales of Japan*

Describing the behavior of wild sea creatures in terms of tame dogs or cats makes these unusual events more ordinary and believable. Readers may be as surprised as Urashima Taro is to discover that the three days he experiences in this magical kingdom were actually 300 years in the real world!

Tips and techniques
Use specific details and everyday comparisons to make magical situations and places seem real to readers.

Be surprising!

You may decide to use comparisons to modern situations to help readers understand an experience unlike their own. This is what Julius Lester does in his retelling of one tale about that mischief-maker Brer [Brother] Rabbit:

Brer Fox and Brer Rabbit were sitting alongside the road one day talking about much of nothing when they heard a strange sound—blim, blim, blim. "What's that?" Brer Fox wanted to know. He didn't know whether to get scared or not.
"That?" answered Brer Rabbit. "Sound like Sister Goose."
"What she be doing?"
"Battling clothes," said Brer Rabbit.
I know y'all don't know what I'm talking about. You take your clothes to the Laundromat, or have a washing machine and dryer sitting right in the house. Way back yonder folks took their clothes down to the creek or stream or what'nsoever, got them real wet, laid 'em across a big rock or something, took a stick and beat the dirt out of them. You don't know nothing about no clean clothes until you put on some what been cleaned with a battlin' stick.
Julius Lester, "How Brer Fox and Brer Dog Became Enemies," in
The Tales of Uncle Remus: The Adventures of Brer Rabbit

Lester speaks directly to modern readers—familiar with Laundromats and washing machines and dryers—to help us understand the old-fashioned way of washing or "battling" clothing by hand.

CASE STUDY

Julius Lester explains why modern devices such as washing machines and Laundromats appear in his folktales. He writes down tales as he would tell them aloud to a modern audience. Lester says that "the storyteller improvises, revitalizing the tale and making it always new."

DISCOVER YOUR HERO

Choose your hero! Many folktales spotlight brave, generous, and kind people. These heroes act properly according to the beliefs of their people, and their virtues bring them rewards.

A few folktale heroes are fools whose greatest gift to readers or listeners is laughter. Other folktales have more complex heroes. They rescue themselves and others by using their wits, but their plans often involve lying or even harming others. Sometimes these mischief-makers outwit themselves! They end up embarrassing or hurting themselves in ridiculous ways.

Tell your hero's problems

Whatever your choice for a hero, your job is to make readers care about this character and his or her problems. Perhaps—like brave Li Chi in a Chinese folktale—your hero willingly risks danger to help her family and village. Li Chi volunteers to meet the hungry serpent that threatens them. She outwits this monster through careful planning as well as bravery. Besides the traditional sword, she brings several unusual tools to help her:

> *The serpent appeared. Its head was as large as a rice barrel; its eyes were like mirrors two feet across. Smelling the fragrance of the rice balls, it opened its mouth to eat them. Then Li Chi unleashed the snake-hunting dog, which bit hard into the serpent. Li Chi came up from behind and scored the serpent with several deep cuts. The wounds hurt so terribly that the monster leaped into the open and died.*
> Jane Yolen, editor, "Li Chi Slays the Serpent," in *Favorite Folktales from Around the World*

For this brave deed, we are told that "ballads celebrating Li Chi survive to this day."

GETTING STARTED	SETTING THE SCENE	CHARACTERS	VIEWPOINT

In Rafe Martin's *The Brave Little Parrot*, a retelling of a tale from India, the hero displays many virtues. She is brave, concerned about other creatures, and determined in her seemingly hopeless struggle to fight a forest fire. The gods respond to her noble efforts by weeping tears that put out the fire. The parrot's virtues are rewarded.

CASE STUDY

Rafe Martin's *The Little Brave Parrot* is part of a long tradition of folktales in India. These stories about animals and other creatures—known as Jataka tales—demonstrate virtues associated with Buddha. He is the central figure in the religion of Buddhism. Jataka tales are also shown in paintings and statues and performed in plays.

Perhaps your hero—like Hungbu in Nina Jaffe's *Older Brother, Younger Brother*—faces a greedy, cruel relative. Hungbu still respects and obeys his older brother and is kind to all living creatures. For maintaining these important traditional Korean virtues, Hungbu and his family receive magical rewards.

CASE STUDY

Nina Jaffe's afterword to *Older Brother, Younger Brother* explains that uncomplaining obedience to older relatives is an important part of Confucianism, a religion in China and Korea.

FOOLISH FOLKTALES

Some folktales are meant mainly to bring laughter.
Their foolish heroes have logic but little common
sense or understanding of the world. Their solutions to
problems are ridiculous, but these heroes are too foolish
to realize this! They remain happy in their ignorance.

Often such tales feature whole towns filled with fools. One
such place in Jewish folktales is the small, imaginary town of
Chelm. In one tale, Chelm's Council of Wise Men decides
to spotlight the wisest man—their Chief
Sage—by giving him golden shoes to wear.
Dirt and mud, though, always hide the
shoes' shiny color. The solution to this
problem is typical of Chelm tales:

> *No one recognized the Chief Sage and
> everyone on the Council of Wise Men was
> in despair. They discussed the problem for
> many days and many nights, and at last
> arrived at a perfect solution. Now, if you go
> to Chelm and walk around, you will know
> at once who the wisest man in the whole
> town is. It's quite clear. He's the one who
> walks about with golden shoes on his hands,
> wearing them as though they were gloves.*
> Adèle Geras, "The Golden
> Shoes," in *My Grandmother's
> Stories: A Collection of Jewish
> Folk Tales*

THREE·WISE·MEN·OF·GO-
-THAM·WENT·TO·SEA·IN·
A·BOWL

The townspeople's happiness
with this silly solution makes
us laugh, but it also has a
serious message. Such folktales
remind their audience that
logic without common sense
can lead to ridiculous results.

CASE STUDY

Other towns filled with fools are found
in folktales around the world. These
funny places include Holmola in Finland
and Gotham in England. Unlike Chelm,
however, these towns really exist—it is just
their foolish inhabitants who are imaginary!

Now it's your turn

Be playful!

Let yourself play with the idea of a town filled with fools. Take 10 minutes in your writing place to brainstorm ideas. You are in for some serious fun! Where would you locate this town? Location affects people's jobs, daily activities, and problems. Would you write about a modern town of fools or about a town in the past? This choice is also important for your story. Once you have answers to these questions, you can begin to jot down problems facing the town's inhabitants. Then you are ready for the next fun-filled step: figuring out silly ways for your foolish heroes to solve these problems!

Find a good name

Some heroes in folktales are already named, but others are not. If you have the chance to name your hero, work some storytelling magic with your choice!

Arthur Ransome retells a Russian tale in *The Fool of the World and the Flying Ship*. Readers never learn the actual name of this fool, whose own family treats him badly. Yet this simple man's determination and kindness to others bring him riches and a princess to marry. By always referring to this hero as "the Fool of the World," Ransome reminds readers that people too often judge others by appearance and fail to recognize someone's true worth. Ransome makes a wise choice by *not* naming the hero here.

Tips and techniques

Even if your hero is not a fool, he or she probably has other weaknesses. No one is perfect! One way to encourage readers to care about your hero is to show this character's flaws.

TRICKSTER HEROES

The many trickster heroes of folktales have strengths that are also sometimes their weaknesses.

In African-American folktales, the most famous tricky hero is Brer Rabbit. The same cleverness, pride, and fighting spirit that help him defeat enemies also get him into trouble. For a while, Brer Rabbit is caught in the tar baby trap that Fox sets for him:

> *"Well, I still got my head," Doc Rabbit said. "I'm mad, now! I'm agone use my head, too."*
> *He used his head on the little tar baby. Butted his head in the tar baby's stomach as hard as he could. Doc Rabbit's head got stuck clear up to his eyes. His big rabbit ears went whole into the tar of Tar Baby.*
> Virginia Hamilton, "Doc Rabbit, Bruh Fox, and Tar Baby," in *The People Could Fly: American Black Folktales*

By the end of this tale, though, Brer Rabbit manages once more to trick Fox and escape.

Not every folktale ends well for the trickster. In Native American stories, this clever character is often known as Coyote. Sometimes he is part of native people's sacred stories, related to their religion. This trickster sometimes means well, but other times he plans harm. If you choose a trickster as your hero, your tale could end well or badly for this character!

CASE STUDY
The wolf or fox is the trickster in many European folktales. In parts of Africa, the spider is the trickster.

Develop a supporting cast

You can tell readers much about your hero and villain by showing how they act with other characters. These exchanges can demonstrate a main character's motives or true nature. Work your storytelling magic by developing a supporting cast of characters.

Rafe Martin's parrot hero does not let the fearful advice of other creatures stop her brave efforts:

> *But the animals huddling on the shore moaned, "There's nothing anyone can do now, little parrot. It's too late."*
> *"It's true," coughed the cheetah. "Fast as I am, the flames are faster."*
> *"And powerful as we are," trumpeted the elephants, "we cannot charge through flames."*
> *"It's hopeless," the animals agreed.*
> Rafe Martin, *The Brave Little Parrot*

By showing how these faster, larger animals have abandoned hope, the author spotlights Little Parrot's inner strength. Readers also learn more about the community of creatures she finally saves.

Tips and techniques
Have other characters tell what your hero looks like. Or have the hero describe his or her own reflection in a mirror, pool, or window.

Now it's your turn

Be heroic!

Use your imagination to brainstorm your hero into being. This exercise works well for any kind of hero—tricksters, fools, and traditionally good figures. Draw five lines down a sheet of paper. Write these words at the top of the six columns: Appearance, Likes, Dislikes, Weaknesses, Strengths, Past Experiences. Now take 10 to 15 minutes to think up five items for each category. You now know 30 things about your hero! You may use all or only some of this information in your tale. Perhaps these ideas will lead you to still more ideas.

CREATE YOUR VILLAIN

Your villain creates the problem or conflict facing the hero. Yet not all villains are evil. This is important to remember as you create a villain who challenges your hero. Sometimes, too, heroes face problems that are outside of human control.

What is the motive?

In folktales, people and creatures commit evil or unpleasant deeds for different reasons. They may be motivated by greed, jealousy, revenge, or even loneliness. They may believe that their deeds are not evil at all, if their society tells them their behavior is correct. Create a believable villain by showing this character's motives.

Some folktale villains

Brutal men who uphold an evil tradition:
The slave owner's white servants beat exhausted black slaves:

> *His Overseer on horseback pointed out the slaves who were slowin down. So the one called Driver cracked his whip over the slow ones to make them move faster. The whip was a slice-open cut of pain. So they did move faster. Had to.*
> Virginia Hamilton, "The People Could Fly," in *The People Could Fly: American Black Folktales*

A relative who ignores tradition and family ties:
Even before he abandons the boy in the forest, his uncle treats him badly:

> *But this boy's uncle did not have a straight mind. Although it was his duty to take care of his nephew, he resented the fact that he had this boy to care for. Instead of taking care of him, he treated him badly. He dressed him in ragged clothes; he gave him only scraps of food to eat; he never even called the boy by his name. He just would say, "Hey, you, get out of my way!"*
> Joseph Bruchac, "The Boy Who Lived With the Bears," in *The Boy Who Lived With the Bears and Other Iroquois Stories*

A natural disaster, such as a drought:

The author uses rhyme to describe these events:

*But one year the rains
were so very belated,
That all of the big wild
creatures migrated.
Then Ki-pat helped to end
that terrible drought—
And this story tells
how it all came about!*
Verna Aardema, *Bringing
the Rain to Kapiti Plain:
A Nandi Tale*

A natural enemy:

In the wild, many creatures survive by eating other animals:

*"Well, I got you now," Brer Fox said
when he was able to catch his breath.
"You floppy-eared, pom-pom-tailed
good-for-nothing! I guess you know who's
having rabbit for dinner this night!"*
Julius Lester, "Brer Rabbit and the Tar
Baby," in *The Tales of Uncle Remus: The
Adventures of Brer Rabbit*

Now it's your turn

The picture of evil

What does your villain look like? If your folktale's villain is human, get ideas by looking through old photographs, magazines, and books. When you find a face that interests you, take five or 10 minutes to write a description of it. Repeat this process. Now reread your descriptions. Is your villain's appearance captured in one description? Perhaps you need to combine descriptions to create your villainous portrait.

CHOOSE A POINT OF VIEW

Before you write the first fantastic line of your **tale, you must decide who is telling its story.**

Do you want readers to know all about the characters—what everyone is thinking, feeling, and doing? Or do you want to follow the thoughts and experiences of just one character—such as your hero? Perhaps you have decided to retell a tale from the viewpoint of several characters. Will you remind readers that people listen to as well as read folktales? These decisions determine your folktale's point of view.

Omniscient viewpoint

Many folktales are told from the all-seeing and all-knowing—the omniscient—point of view. The storyteller or narrator describes what all the characters think and feel and also shares knowledge of events beyond the characters' knowledge. Such

tales often begin with or include the words "long ago" in their opening remarks. That is how this folktale about storytelling begins:

> *Long, long ago, when the earth was set down and the sky was lifted up, all folktales were owned by the Sky God.*
> Verna Aardema, *Anansi Does the Impossible! An Ashanti Tale*

Many folktales, even ones told from the omniscient viewpoint, also remind readers that stories are passed down from one generation to the next. The words "They say," "It is said," or "It is told" also appear in the tale's beginning. That is how this tale about a forgetful chief begins:

> *This story happened long ago, when, it is told, the people of Ono Island had a chief named Tui Matakono.*
> Nina Jaffe, "The Silent Drum of Ono Island," in *Patakin: World Tales of Drums and Drummers*

Most storytellers use this tale-telling tradition to support the truth of the coming tale.

First-person viewpoint

The first-person viewpoint uses a character in the tale to narrate the story. This narrator uses words such as "I said," "I thought," or "I did." In folktales, the narrator giving us his or her own viewpoint is often the storyteller. That person may break into the story to comment on the events. That is what happens in this tale about Brer Rabbit:

> "How you today, Sister Goose?"
> "Just fine, Brer Rabbit. Excuse me for not shaking hands with you, but I got all these suds on my hands."
> Brer Rabbit said he understood.
> I suppose I got to stop the story, 'cause I can hear you thinking that a goose don't have hands. And next thing I know you be trying to get me to believe that snakes don't have feet and cats don't have wings, and I know better! So, if you don't mind, you can keep your thought to yourself and I'll get back to the story.
> Julius Lester, "How Brer Fox and Brer Dog Became Enemies," in *The Tales of Uncle Remus: The Adventures of Brer Rabbit*

By inserting such playful first-person remarks into a tale that otherwise has an omniscient viewpoint, Julius Lester jokes with readers. He interacts with them in the way a storyteller would with a live audience—sharing the humor in ridiculous ideas about creatures.

CASE STUDY

Joel Chandler Harris first collected and published Brer Rabbit folktales in the late 19th century. Harris used a narrator he called Uncle Remus to tell these African-American folktales. Modern versions of these tales often omit Uncle Remus and change the language Harris used. Many people feel that Harris' version of these tales was not true-to-life.

THIRD-PERSON VIEWPOINT

With the third-person viewpoint, the writer stays inside one character's mind but uses "he said" or "she thought" to describe events. This narrator can only tell what other characters think or feel through dialogue.

Sometimes this narrating character is not as clever as he thinks! In one Vietnamese folktale, a greedy rich man believes he does not have to keep his bargain with a poor but clever boy. The only witness to their agreement is a fly. After all, the man thought "the little genius still had much to learn, believing that a fly could be a witness for anybody." Yet the rich man's own words betray him when a judge hears this case. The boy speaks first:

> *"Yes, Your Honor, a fly. A fly which was alighting on this gentleman's nose!" The boy leaped from his seat.*
> *"Insolent little devil, that's a pack of lies!" The rich man roared indignantly, his face like a ripe tomato. "The fly was not on my nose; he was on the housepole ..." But he stopped dead. It was, however, too late.*
> Jane Yolen, editor, "The Fly," in *Favorite Folktales from Around the World*

Even the rich man finally laughs at himself when he realizes his mistake. The clever boy has tricked him, and the judge orders the man to pay his debt.

Multiple third-person viewpoint

Using multiple third-person points of view adds drama to your folktale. In *The Brave Little Parrot*, the author shifts between the parrot's viewpoint and that of the god who comes to admire her. Changing into an eagle to follow the parrot, this god weeps tears that put out the forest fire.

In her West African folktale explaining *Why Mosquitoes Buzz in People's Ears,* Verna Aardema adds excitement and humor by giving the viewpoints of eight creatures! Since each of them only knows his or her own part of the tale, King Lion calls a meeting of all the creatures to figure out what has happened. To the surprise of everyone, it is the tiny mosquito who started a chain of misunderstandings and unpleasant events.

Now it's your turn

Visit another viewpoint!

Think of a scene in your tale where the hero first meets or finally fights the villain. Write this scene from the hero's point of view. Now use the bridge of your imagination to explore another viewpoint. Write this scene again from the villain's point of view. Magically switch viewpoints again to rewrite this scene from the sidelines, using the viewpoint of a nearby person or animal. Reread your scenes. Which version do you like best? Perhaps you will end up using more than one point of view in your tale. Allow half an hour for this activity.

TELL YOUR STORY'S STORY

As your folktale takes shape like a basket handcrafted by a great weaver, it is a good idea to describe it in a paragraph or two. This is called a synopsis.

If someone asked, "What is this folktale about?" your synopsis would be the answer. An editor often wants to see a synopsis of a story before accepting it for publication.

Study back cover blurbs

Studying the information on the back cover of a book—called the blurb—will help you write an effective synopsis. A good blurb contains a brief summary of a book's content. It also gives the tone of the book—whether it is serious or funny. Most important of all, the blurb makes readers want to open the book and read it cover-to-cover! That is true of this blurb:

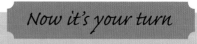
Now it's your turn

Announce it with flair!
Write a blurb for the folktale you plan to write. Summarizing it in one or two paragraphs will sharpen your ideas.

The Sky God rubbed his great chin. At last he said, "The price is three impossible tasks. Bring me a live python, a real fairy, and forty-seven stinging hornets."
Verna Aardema, *Anansi Does the Impossible! An Ashanti Tale*

Make a story map

One way to plan your folktale is to think of it the way filmmakers prepare a movie. They must know the main story episodes before the cameras start shooting. Before they start filming, filmmakers map out the plot (the sequence of events) in a series of sketches called storyboards. You can do this for your folktale. The blurb you wrote will help you here.

Now it's your turn

Lights! Camera! Action!

Reread your blurb. Use it to identify the most important events in the folktale. You are now ready to sketch the "scenes" for the tale's story. Under each sketched scene, jot down brief notes about what you will mention about this event. Use this series of storyboards as a helpful outline as you write the tale. If your

retelling of this tale has chapters, each scene may be a separate chapter. Perhaps two or more scenes will fit together well in one chapter.

Write a chapter synopsis

Another way to plan a longer work is to write a chapter synopsis. If your folktale will be a chapter book, this method might help you tell it. Group major events into four to eight categories. Then plan the plot of each category or chapter. Each chapter will have its own beginning, middle, and end. Your hero will encounter a villain and face a conflict.

Think about your theme

As you plan your scenes, think about your folktale's theme. Folktales traditionally contain messages about the right way to behave. Will your tale be about obedience and kindness, like Nina Jaffe's *Older Brother, Younger Brother*? Perhaps it will be about courage and determination, like Rafe Martin's *The Brave Little Parrot*. What messages about good or bad behavior does your folktale send readers?

BAIT THE HOOK

You have planned your plot, and you are now ready to delight readers with your folktale. What storyteller's lure will you use to capture their attention?

Folktale beginnings

Many folktales open immediately with events in the story. *Older Brother, Younger Brother* and Katherine Paterson's *The Tale of the Mandarin Ducks* begin this way. Some folktales, however, begin with an author's note telling about the people whose tale this is. Joseph Bruchac gives such information in the first pages of *The Boy Who Lived With the Bears and Other Iroquois Stories.* Other folktales begin with a glossary that defines native words used in the tale. Verna Aardema starts *Anansi Does the Impossible!* that way.

After any special introductions such as these, get ready to grab and hold on to your readers' attention. Your tale's opening sentences are important. They are the hook that will reel readers into your folktale world.

Tips and techniques
Try out different openings for your tale. Just like actors, storytellers often "rehearse" the tales they tell before they perform for a live audience.

Attention-grabbing openings:

Here are examples of sentences that capture readers in a web of storytelling magic:

A mysterious opening filled with vivid descriptions:

They say the people could fly. Say that long ago in Africa, some of the people knew magic. And they would walk up on the air like climbin up on a gate. And they flew like blackbirds over the fields. Black, shiny wings flappin against the blue up there.
Virginia Hamilton, "The People Could Fly," in *The People Could Fly: American Black Folktales*

A traditional opening used for all of a people's tales:

> "We do not mean, we do not really mean, that everything you're about to hear is the truth. A story, a story! Let it come, let it go!
> Nina Jaffe, "Anansi and the Secret Name," in *Patakin: World Tales of Drums and Drummers*

A vivid beginning that speaks directly to the reader:

> *In the High and Far-Off Times, the Elephant, O Best Beloved, had no trunk. He had only a blackish, bulgy nose, as big as a boot, that he could wriggle about from side to side; but he couldn't pick up things with it.*
> Rudyard Kipling, "The Elephant's Child," in *Just So Stories*

CASE STUDY

The "Best Beloved" in Rudyard Kipling's *Just So Stories* is his daughter Josephine (left). The young girl died of pneumonia in 1899, three years before Kipling published these tales, which he had created to entertain Josephine and her sister. Kipling was influenced by the many talking beast folktales of India, where he and his family then lived.

BUILD THE SUSPENSE

After your wonderful opening, you must not let your audience's attention wander. Keep and build suspense for readers by showing the hero's adventures and using a variety of storytelling techniques.

Tips and techniques
Imitate the drumlike rhythm of spoken folktales. Create and repeat a phrase that describes the setting or hero. Use words inside this phrase that have similar sounds.

Create a storytelling rhythm

Storytellers who speak, sing, or chant their tales often use drums or other musical instruments. This tradition adds a compelling, exciting rhythm to these tales. Some writers of folktales imitate this drumbeat by repeating an unusual phrase throughout a tale. Often the sounds of the words there pound one after the other like a hand thumping a drum. In "The Elephant's Child," Rudyard Kipling repeats the words "the great, grey-green, greasy Limpopo River." Soon readers begin to anticipate this phrase.

A number of adventures

Because people long ago believed that the numbers three and seven had magical significance, these numbers appear in many European tales. Heroes often face three dangers or obstacles to overcome. Sometimes they also have three or seven magical helpers, too. This is the situation facing the Fool of the World in Arthur Ransome's tale. If you wish, follow this folktale tradition and plot out three or seven exciting adventures for your hero.

Tips and techniques
Start small and build up to the most challenging adventures for your hero. This will keep readers from feeling let down.

Use dramatic irony

When readers know something the characters do not, suspense increases. This situation is called dramatic irony. One way to create dramatic irony is through dialogue. This technique is effective in an old folktale about six blind men encountering an elephant for the first time:

> *The fourth blind man put out his hand and touched the leg of the elephant. "How tall! An elephant is like a tree."*
> *The fifth blind man reached out his hand and touched the ear of the elephant. "How wide! An elephant is like a fan."*
> Lillian Quigley, *The Blind Men and the Elephant: An Old Tale From the Land of India*

We know how wrong each man's opinion is, but they do not. Suspense increases as their mistakes continue, and we wait to see if and how they will learn the truth.

END WITH A BANG

Stories build up suspense until they reach a climax. After this dramatic point, the characters' main problems are solved. In some folktales, the hero has learned something or earned a reward. In others, a villain is punished and learns a lesson. In tales where a trickster is punished, the character may or may not learn a lesson.

The climax

A folktale's climax is often very dramatic. It tops off the suspense with a scene where action produces strong emotions in the characters. In "The Boy Who Lived With the Bears," the climax occurs when the boy protects his bear family from a dangerous hunter. Only after Boy shouts, "Stop! Don't hurt my family!" does he learn that this hunter is the uncle who abandoned him. In *The Tale of the Mandarin Ducks*, the climax occurs when two kind servants think they will die but are mysteriously rescued in the ducks' forest home.

Conclude your adventure

Have your hero finish his or her adventure. Like Hungbu in *Older Brother, Younger Brother*, this result may be a happy, contented life. For a trickster like Coyote, though, the result may be disappointing. In one tale by Janet Stevens, Coyote tries to become young again by tricking other creatures out of their strength. His attempts continually disappoint and even injure him.

Yet Coyote does not learn his lesson. The tale ends with Coyote howling out to Young Elk: "You certainly are big, powerful, young, and strong. How about sharing some of your power with an old bag of bones like me?" Readers then may well laugh at Coyote for believing that this attempt will have a better result.

CASE STUDY

Sometimes writers of folktales include information about how they first heard a tale in an afterword. Virginia Hamilton and Nina Jaffe often do this. Other authors, such as Rafe Martin in *The Brave Little Parrot*, use an afterword to provide information about the people whose tale they are retelling.

Endings that suggest new beginnings

A good ending often refers back in some way to the beginning of the story. This reminds readers of how much has or has not changed since the tale started. In "The Boy Who Drew Cats," the title character at first gets into trouble for his drawing. Later his skillfully drawn cats save him from rat goblins! By the end of the tale, this boy's life has changed dramatically, but his interests remain the same:

> *In time the boy became a great artist known through-*
> *out the islands of Japan.*
> *But it's said no matter how great he became, every day*
> *he took out his ink stick, poured water on his grinding*
> *stone, ground up his ink, dipped in his brush, and drew at least one cat.*
> Rafe Martin, "The Boy Who Drew Cats," in *Mysterious Tales of Japan*

In *Older Brother, Younger Brother*, the happy ending extends beyond obedient Hungbu and his brother, who finally learns kindness, to later generations:

> *Through all the changing seasons until the end of their days,*
> *Hungbu and Nolbu, younger brother and older brother, lived*
> *together in peace and harmony in the house on the mountainside*
> *that the swallow's gift had brought. And so did their children and*
> *grandchildren and all their descendents to this very day.*
> Nina Jaffe, *Older Brother, Younger Brother: A Korean Folktale*

Bad endings

To create a folktale that leaves readers feeling satisfied, avoid a bad ending. Bad endings are ones that:

- fizzle out or end abruptly because you've run out of ideas
- fail to show how the characters have changed or reacted to events in some way
- are too grim and depressing and leave readers with no hope

CHAPTER 6: WINNING WORDS

MAKE WORDS WORK

Your well-chosen words
will work wonders. They
will transport readers to
distant times and places
where unusual events and
characters such as Urashima
Taro seem as real as next-
door neighbors.

Every word counts. Just as you would
not waste water in a desert, choose your
words wisely. Only the most vivid and
powerful words are worthy of your tale.

A sense of life

Use as many of the five senses as possible
to make descriptions come alive. Here
the writer uses sound, smell, touch, and
sight to communicate the character's
impressions of a flower shop:

*[W]e chose what we wanted: pale pink gladioli, perhaps, so
tall that they seemed to me like thin tree branches waving
above my head, or red carnations, or the tightly curled-up
buds of yellow roses. I loved to watch Moshe take the flowers
and wrap them in whispery sheets of paper and tie a beautiful ribbon around the stems. The shop smelled green and
moist. It smelled of earth and moss and fern and hundreds
and hundreds of flowers. In summer, Moshe kept the shut-
ters closed to protect the flowers from the sun, and stepping
into the shop was like entering a cool, dark cave.*
Adèle Geras, "The Garden of Talking Flowers," in *My
Grandmother's Stories: A Collection of Jewish Folk Tales*

Tips and techniques

A metaphor describes something by calling it something else—for instance, a fierce man is a "tiger." A simile describes something by comparing it to something with the word "like" or "as." For example, a dewdrop sparkles like a diamond.

Use vivid imagery

Use your imagination to create vivid word pictures with metaphors and similes. In "The People Could Fly," the storyteller uses metaphors to describe the slave owner's lack of human feelings:

The slaves labored in the fields from sunup to sundown. The owner of the slaves callin himself their Master. Say he was a hard lump of clay. A hard, glinty coal. A hard rock pile, wouldn't be moved.
Virginia Hamilton, "The People Could Fly," in *The People Could Fly: American Black Folktales*

This does not mean that this man's body was made of stone instead of flesh. It is a word picture that communicates that human emotions had no effect on him—just as they do not affect clay, coal, or rock.

In a Papago tale from the American Southwest, Joseph Bruchac uses similes to describe butterflies:

The children opened Elder Brother's bag and out of it flew the first butterflies. Their wings were bright as sunlight and held all of the colors of the flowers and the leaves, the cornmeal, the pollen and the green pine needles. They were red and gold and black and yellow, blue and green and white. They looked like flowers, dancing in the wind.
Joseph Bruchac, "How the Butterflies Came to Be," in *Native American Animal Stories*

These word pictures comparing butterflies to sunlight and flowers help readers imagine the butterflies' intense colors and graceful movement.

WRITE TO EXCITE

When you write action scenes, excite your readers with your word choice. Replace everyday action words with bold, unusual ones. Have characters zoom instead of run, and glide instead of walk.

Rafe Martin uses vivid action words along with metaphors to describe the struggles of the brave little parrot:

Flames leaped at her. Fierce heat struck and thick smoke coiled. Walls of fire shot up now on one side, now on the other. But twisting and turning through the mad maze of fire, the little parrot flew bravely on.
Rafe Martin, *The Brave Little Parrot*

Instead of *rose*, Martin uses the more exciting words *leaped*, *struck*, and *coiled*. The fire is so thick it is a wall and so confusing to fly through that it is a maze.

Now it's your turn

Imagine that!
Brainstorm some similes for colors and textures. Make a list of 10 colors and textures. For each word, write down five similes. For instance, "As yellow (or gray or green) as a …" Or try "As smooth (or sharp or rough) as the …" How could you use these images or ones like them in your folktale? Use a dictionary or thesaurus for extra help.

Tips and techniques
Do not let the length of a chapter book discourage you from starting one. If you have many tales to tell about one character or a group of characters, these ideas may inspire you. Completing a chapter book may be no more work than writing just one excellent action-filled tale.

Now it's your turn

Act up!
By yourself or with a friend, make a list of 10 everyday action words such as *walk* or *fly* or *run*. Then have fun brainstorming at least four unusual substitutes for each word. Perhaps a villain would skulk instead of hide. Use a dictionary or thesaurus for extra help.

USE DRAMATIC DIALOGUE

Conversations can help readers understand different personalities and the relationships among people. Dialogue

also gives readers' eyes a rest as it breaks up the page of narrative (storytelling). Done well, dialogue is a powerful storytelling tool— one that adds color, mood, and suspense even as it moves the plot forward.

Let your characters speak for themselves

After their father's death, the elder brother of this folktale reveals his selfish, cruel nature while the younger one continues to be obedient and good-natured:

> *After the funeral and the days of mourning were over, Nolbu called his brother into the courtyard.*
> *"As you know, my dear younger brother, our father left this house and everything in it to me, for I am the oldest. I'm tired of having you and your family around, eating up all our food and crowding into every room in the house. Be off with you!" he said spitefully. "And don't bother to come back!"*
> *Hungbu nodded. "It shall be as you wish, my brother."*
> Nina Jaffe, *Older Brother, Younger Brother: A Korean Folktale*

Nolbu's selfish act is an important plot element in this tale.

Now it's your turn

Listen in

Tune in to the way people talk. Turn on the TV or radio for 10 minutes, and copy down bits of conversation. Or jot down what you overhear on a train or in an elevator or at school. You will begin to notice how people often have favorite expressions and different rhythms to their speech. Sometimes someone may not wait to talk until the other person is finished. How can you use these different speech patterns in the dialogue you write?

Follow convention

Dialogue is usually written according to certain rules. Each new speaker begins a new paragraph. You already know that what a person actually said is enclosed in quotation marks, followed or preceded by a tag such as "he said" or "she said." Sometimes, to give the sense of a real conversation, writers place these tags in the middle of a sentence. This placement adds another rhythm to the conversation, making it more lifelike.

Tips and techniques
Use say, said, or wrote to introduce quotations. Sometimes substitute words such as complained, whispered, or shouted for variety and when they suit the situation.

ADDING COLOR AND MOOD

Adèle Geras used dialogue to add color and mood to her story about poor people outwitting rich, powerful ones.

In the folktale she retells, a farmer named Frankel outsmarts the Czar, the ruler of Russia. This powerful man is angry because Frankel seems to have broken a promise, but the fact that the Czar's picture is on valuable Russian coins complicates things:

> *Well, eventually, the Police brought Frankel to see the Czar.*
> *"What have you to say for yourself, you wretch?" yelled the Czar. "Did you not promise me that you would not reveal the secret you told me?"*
> *"I said," Frankel whispered, "that I would only reveal it after I had seen your face a hundred times."*
> *"But this is only the second time you have seen me, you worm! What have you to say for yourself before I have you shot?"*
> *Forgive me, Czar," said Frankel, and he took out the bag containing the hundred silver rubles which the chancellors had given him. "Here are one hundred coins. I have looked at every one. Therefore, I'm sure you will agree, I have seen your face one hundred times."*
> Adele Geras, "The Face of the Czar," in *My Grandmother's Stories: A Collection of Jewish Folk Tales*

Although the sly way that Frankel gets around his promise to the Czar is funny, his trick has a surprisingly serious and good outcome. The Czar is so impressed by Frankel's cleverness that he makes the farmer his new chief adviser!

CASE STUDY

Family gatherings inspired Rafe Martin's interest in stories using dialogue. At holidays, he writes, "Stories were hardly ever told by one person. Everyone interrupted everyone else, throwing in pieces, details, and changes so that the stories grew, with each person throwing something of their own into the pot."

Now it's your turn

Compress your dialogue

Try removing tags such as "he said" or "she shouted" from your dialogue. Does the pace of the conversation seem more natural? Does this pace better suit the mood and purpose of the scene? Can you still identify who is speaking? Some scenes work better with com-

pressed dialogue that has no tags. If you cannot tell who is speaking without tags, you may want to work more to develop each character's voice.

Tips and techniques

Use italics for words that characters emphasize in their speech, and use capital letters for words that they shout.

Now it's your turn

As she was saying ...

Reread your folktale. Are there parts of the narrative that could be better told in dialogue? Rewrite a scene using or adding dialogue. If it is appropriate, use humor in a conversation between characters or have them interrupt or talk over each other. Now set both versions of the tale aside. Go back later and see which version you like more.

USE DIFFERENT VOICES

Writing dialogue is a challenge even for experienced, skilled writers. Remember that characters should not sound like you! How characters speak often reveals a great deal about their background.

Here are examples of how people's speech differs in vocabulary, rhythm, accent, and pronunciation.

A combination of cultures:

Anansi and his wife, Aso, include Ashanti words in their English speech. *Pesa* is like the English *psst* for a whispering sound. *Ghe* is like *ha-ha* for a laughing noise:

Tips and techniques

Watch out! Your slang may not fit well into a folktale set long ago or far away.

Anansi ran home to Aso and asked, "How are we going to catch forty-seven hornets?" Aso thought and thought. Finally, she said, "I know how!" And she whispered, pesa, pesa, pesa, to Anansi.
Anansi laughed, ghe, ghe, ghe!
Verna Aardema, *Anansi Does the Impossible! An Ashanti Tale*

Wordplay that shows a character's sense of humor:

By making up new words, Young Buffalo mocks foolish Coyote's attempt to regain his youth:

When the dust cleared, Young Buffalo said, "Open your eyes, Coyote." Coyote looked at himself. He had changed into a young buffalo! "Yippee," he snorted. "I'm young again."
"That's right," said Buffalo. "But remember, Coyote, even though most of you looks like a young Buffalo on the outside, on the inside you are still a powerless coyote. See, I left your coyote tail to remind you. You are a coyo-talo! Or maybe a buffote. Let's call you that—a buff-OH-tee. Don't forget that a buffote has no power or you'll get into trouble. Now, be off with you!"
Janet Stevens, *Old Bag of Bones: A Coyote Tale*

A speech defect caused by an attack:

Captured Elephant's Child cannot pronounce words correctly:

> *Then the Elephant's Child put his head down*
> *close to the Crocodile's musky, tusky mouth, and the*
> *Crocodile caught him by his little nose, which up to*
> *that very week, day, hour, and minute, had been no*
> *bigger than a boot, though much more useful.*
> *"I think," said the Crocodile—and he said it*
> *between his teeth, like this—"I think to-day I*
> *will begin with Elephant's Child!"*
> *At this, O Best Beloved, the Elephant's Child was*
> *much annoyed, and he said, speaking through*
> *his nose, like this, "Led go! You are hurtig be!"*
> Rudyard Kipling, "The Elephant's Child,"
> in *Just So Stories*

A dialect of English:

The storyteller and characters in this tale use the rhythm and expressions of speech of African-Americans in the southern United States:

> *And that's what Brother Fox did. He sure did. Took Doc Rabbit by the*
> *short hair and threw him—Whippit! Whappit!—right in the briar patch.*
> *"Hot lettuce pie! This is where I want to be," Doc Rabbit hollered for*
> *happiness. He was square in the middle of the briar patch. "Here is*
> *where my mama and papa had me born and raised. Safe at last!"*
> Virginia Hamilton, "Doc Rabbit, Bruh Fox, and Tar Baby,"
> in *The People Could Fly: American Black Folktales*

Speech that reflects a creature's real-life sounds:

The talking snake of this Jataka tale hisses like ordinary snakes:

> *"What?" said the snake. "The earth'sss breaking up? Why I'd better*
> *get sssliding." And uncoiling himself, he glided down from his warm*
> *ledge and slid rapidly after the others.*
> Rafe Martin, *Foolish Rabbit's Big Mistake*

BEAT WRITER'S BLOCK

Even talented pro-**f**essional writers are sometimes silenced by writer's block. That is when a writer is stuck for words or ideas at the beginning or in the middle of a story. Never fear! There are ways to regain your storyteller's voice—and they work like a fine folk remedy!

Tips and techniques
To get fresh ideas, take a break in a different environment to think through a writing problem. Or just take a break!

Ignore your inner critic

If you have been following the writer's golden rule (writing regularly and often), you already have a powerful weapon against writer's block. But whatever you do, do NOT listen to that inner critic that might be whispering negative ideas about your writing. All writers experience some failures and rejection. Adèle Geras' first picture books were rejected for two years. Katherine Paterson realizes that "it takes courage to lay your insides out for people to examine. … But that's the only way to give what is your unique gift to the world." She urges every new writer to "send your inner critic off on vacation and just write the way little children play."

If someone believes that your tale needs rewriting, do not be discouraged. Rafe Martin says he "rewrite[s] many times. Ten or twenty times with each story is pretty usual. Rewriting is a way of going deeper into the story and your imagining it." He adds that "writers don't rewrite because their first effort was wrong. They rewrite so the story can grow slowly into itself. It is a magical and mysterious process."

Now it's your turn

A character-building activity

Stuck in the middle of your story? Try getting to know your characters better. Ask yourself what makes a character angry, happy, or embarrassed. Now have this character write you a letter complaining about the story or the other characters!

Learn the tricks of the trade

A writers' group

Writing may seem lonely. Some writers find that the cure for this problem is belonging to a writers' group. They meet regularly in person or over the Internet with "writing buddies." These critique groups help fight writer's block by sharing ideas, experiences, and even goals. While Adèle Geras has never belonged to a formal writers' group, she discusses writing problems and exchanges ideas with friends.

Role-play

Another way to beat loneliness as a writer is to involve your family or friends. Turn your writing problem into a game with them. Give each person a character role from your story, and see what ideas and dialogue turn up.

NOW WHAT?

Congratulations! Completing your own folktale is a great achievement. You have learned a lot about writing and probably about yourself, too. You are now ready to take the next step in creating wonderful new stories.

Another folktale?

While writing this folktale, you might have had ideas for another one. Perhaps you told your first tale from the hero's point of view but now want to try one told by a minor character. Perhaps you want to tell a tale set in a different culture or part of the world.

How about a sequel?

Is there more to tell about the characters in your completed folktale? Maybe further adventures await them. This is especially true of tricksters, who always seem to have more mischief in them. Joseph Bruchac continues to gather and retell Native American stories, some of which have the same characters.

Now it's your turn

Imagine that!

Brainstorm your next story with pencil and paper. Think of a folktale you enjoyed reading. List five things that might have happened to the hero or creatures after or even before the events described in the tale. Do not worry about punctuation or grammar as you jot down ideas. Repeat this process with another tale. When you are done, you may have found the characters and plot for your next writing project.

Tips and techniques

Get inspiration and new ideas by examining different versions of the same folktale. For example, look at the different ways that Virginia Hamilton and Julius Lester tell the tale of Brer Rabbit and the Tar Baby. Or compare this African-American tale to the Apache story "Coyote Fights a Lump of Pitch" in Favorite Folktales From Around the World.

LEARN FROM THE AUTHORS

You can learn a great deal from the advice of successful writers. Almost all will tell you that success without hard work and occasional failure is just an "old wives' tale"! Yet even though few writers earn enough from their books to make a living, they value their ability to create and communicate through written words.

Julius Lester

Julius Lester hosted radio and TV talk shows before he became a writer. He says, "I write because there is something I want to know and the only way I can find out is to write about it." When asked where ideas for his books come from, Lester says, "I don't get ideas as much as I get a feeling and want to know more about that feeling. I spend a lot of time wondering what it's like to be someone I see on the street, or what it was like to have been alive at a certain time in history, or what it's like to have something happen to you. Writing comes as much from the heart as it does the head." He reminds young writers that "the majority of writers do not make a lot of money from writing. If you want to make a lot of money, you shouldn't be a writer."

CASE STUDY

Professional authors fight and win the battle against writer's block, too. Katherine Paterson says, "You can't wait for inspiration to strike. It's like lightning. Hardly ever does it twice in the same book." She recommends that "you go to work every morning." Joseph Bruchac has similar advice for young writers. He tells them to "forget about writer's block. Just sit down and start writing and sooner or later you'll find something worth saying." Julius Lester is content when he reaches his personal goal of completing three pages in a day. Many writers find that taking a break for a walk or some exercise sometimes helps shake off writer's block.

Nina Jaffe

As a girl, Nina Jaffe loved reading folktales and myths. She grew up on the Lower East Side of New York City, an area filled with immigrants speaking many languages. For her, folktales were another way "to get to know about people" from different backgrounds. Jaffe began to write after her son was born. She believes that "storytelling and writing are a way of connecting; of passing on wisdom, knowledge and understanding that have been part of human history and civilization for many centuries." She adds that "these stories come through my own voice, my own imagination, but they are also part of other people's lives and histories. It's wonderful to think that stories will continue to be told and retold, as I put them into written form."

PREPARE YOUR WORK

Let your folktale rest in your desk or on a shelf for several weeks. Then when you read it through, you will have fresh eyes to spot any flaws.

Edit your work

Reading your work aloud is one way to make the writing crisper. Now is the time to check spelling and punctuation. When the tale is as good as it can be, write it out again or type it up on the computer. This is your manuscript.

Be professional

If you have a computer, you can type up your manuscript to give it a professional presentation. Manuscripts should always be printed on one side of white paper, with wide margins and double spacing. Pages should be numbered, and each chapter should start on a new page. You should also include your title as a header on the top of each page. At the front, you should have a title page with your name, address, telephone number, and e-mail address on it.

Make your own book

If your school has its own computer lab, why not use it to publish your folktale? Using a computer allows you to choose your own font (print style) or justify the text (making margins even, like some professionally printed pages). When you have typed and saved the folktale to a file, you can edit it quickly with the spelling and grammar checker, or move sections around using the cut-and-paste tool, which saves a lot of rewriting. A graphics program will let you design and print a cover for the book, too.

Having the folktale on a computer file also means you can print a copy whenever you need one or revise the whole tale if you want to.

Tips and techniques
Great titles capture the reader's interest. They not only indicate the subject of the book but also make the reader want to learn more about it.

Tips and techniques
Always make a copy of your folktale before you give it to others to read. Otherwise, if they lose it, you may have lost all your valuable work.

REACH YOUR AUDIENCE

The next step is to find an audience for your tale. Family members or classmates may be receptive. Members of a community group such as a Girl Scout troop, a local historical society, or a senior citizens' center might like to read your work. Or you may want to share your work through a Web site, a literary magazine, or a publishing house.

Some places to publish your folktale

There are several magazines and writing Web sites that accept folktales from young authors. Some give writing advice and run regular competitions. Each site has its own rules about submitting work, so remember to read these carefully. Here are two more ideas:

- Send the folktale to your school newspaper.
- Watch your local newspaper or magazines for writing competitions you could enter.

Finding a publisher

Study the market to find out which publishers publish folktales. Addresses of publishers and information about whether they accept submissions can be found in writers' handbooks in your local library. Remember that manuscripts that haven't been asked for or paid for by a publisher—called unsolicited manuscripts—are rarely published. Secure any submission with a staple or paper clip, and always enclose a short letter (explaining what you have sent) and a self-addressed, stamped envelope for the tale's return.

Writer's tip

Don't lose heart if an editor rejects your folktale. See this as a chance to make your work better and try again. Remember, having your work published is a wonderful thing, but it is not the only thing. Being able to write a folktale is an accomplishment that will delight the people you love. Talk about it with your younger brother or sister. Read it to your grandfather. Find your audience.

Some final words

You are now a member of a great storytelling tradition. People around the world for generations have told folktales. You have shown that you too can write an entertaining tale that captures people's hearts and minds while teaching important lessons. With this success, you are ready to set out on the next exciting adventure in your life!

Read! Write!

And keep your sense of fun and excitement alive.

Glossary

chapter synopsis—an outline that describes briefly what happens in a chapter

dramatic irony—when the reader knows something the characters do not

edit—to remove all unnecessary words from your story, correct errors, and rewrite the text until the story is the best it can be

editor—the person at a publishing house who finds new books to publish and advises authors on how to improve their stories by telling them what needs to be added or cut

first-person viewpoint—a viewpoint that allows a single character to tell the story as if he or she had written it; readers feel as if that character is talking directly to them

manuscript—a book or article typed or written by hand

metaphor—a figure of speech that paints a word picture; calling a man "a mouse" is a metaphor from which we learn in one word that the man is timid or weak, not that he is actually a mouse

motives—the reasons a character does something

narrative—the telling of a story

omniscient viewpoint—the viewpoint of an all-seeing narrator who can describe all the characters and tell readers how they are acting and feeling

plot—the sequence of events that drive a story forward; the problems that the hero must resolve

point of view—the eyes through which a story is told

prequel—an account of events that occur to characters before they appear in an existing story

publishers—individuals or companies that pay for an author's manuscript to be printed as a book and that distribute and sell that book

sequel—a story that carries an existing one forward

simile—saying something is like something else; a word picture, such as "clouds like frayed lace"

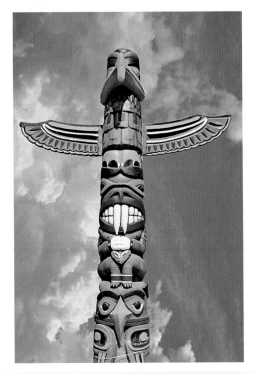

synopsis—a short summary that describes what a story is about and introduces the main characters

theme—the main issue that the story addresses, such as good versus evil, the importance of truth, and so on; a story can have more than one theme

third-person viewpoint—a viewpoint that describes the events of the story through one character's eyes

trickster—a cunning character in folktales—often an animal—who solves problems through wit; a trickster's mischief sometimes harms the trickster as well as others

unsolicited manuscripts—manuscripts that are sent to publishers without being requested; these submissions usually end up in the "slush pile," where they may wait a long time to be read

writer's block—when writers think they can no longer write or have used up all their ideas

FURTHER INFORMATION

Further information

Visit your local libraries and make friends with the librarians. They can direct you to useful sources of information, including magazines that publish young people's folktales. You can learn your craft and read great stories at the same time.

Librarians also know whether any storytellers are scheduled to speak in your area. Many authors visit schools and offer writing workshops. Ask your teacher to invite an author to speak at your school.

On the Web

For more information on this topic, use FactHound.
1. Go to *www.facthound.com*
2. Type in this book ID: 0756535166
3. Click on the *Fetch It* button.
FactHound will find the best Web sites for you.

Read all the Write Your Own books

Write Your Own Adventure Story
Write Your Own Autobiography
Write Your Own Biography
Write Your Own Fairy Tale
Write Your Own Fantasy Story
Write Your Own Folktale
Write Your Own Historical Fiction Story
Write Your Own Legend
Write Your Own Mystery Story
Write Your Own Myth
Write Your Own Poetry
Write Your Own Realistic Fiction Story
Write Your Own Science Fiction Story
Write Your Own Tall Tale

Read more folktales

Abrahams, Roger D. *Afro American Folktales: Stories from Black Traditions in the New World*. New York: Pantheon Books, 1985.

Ada, Alma Flor. *The Rooster Who Went to His Uncle's Wedding: A Latin American Folktale*. New York: Putnam, 1993.

Arnold, Katya. *Baba Yaga and the Little Girl: A Russian Folktale*. New York: North-South Books, 1994.

Birdseye, Tom. *Soap! Soap! Don't Forget the Soap! An Appalachian Folktale*. New York: Holiday House, 1993.

Brett, Jan. *The Mitten: A Ukrainian Folktale*. New York: Putnam, 1989.

Bushnaq, Inea. *Arab Folktales*. New York: Pantheon Books, 1986.

Chase, Richard. *Grandfather Tales: American-English Folk Tales*. Boston: Houghton Mifflin, 2003.

Chase, Richard. *Jack and the Three Sillies*. Boston: Houghton Mifflin, 1950.

Cohn, Amy L. *From Sea to Shining Sea: A Treasury of American Folklore and Folk Songs*. New York: Scholastic, 1993.

Cole, Joanna. *Best-Loved Folktales of the World*. Garden City, N.Y.: Doubleday, 1982.

Keams, Geri. *Grandmother Spider Brings the Sun: A Cherokee Story*. Flagstaff, Ariz.: Northland Pub., 1995.

Lester, Julius. *The Last Tales of Uncle Remus*. New York: Dial, 1994.

Lobel, Arnold. *Ming Lo Moves the Mountain*. New York: Mulberry Books, 1993.

Lurie, Alison. *Clever Gretchen and Other Forgotten Folktales*. New York: Crowell, 1980.

MacDonald, Margaret Read. *Peace Tales: World Folktales to Talk About*. Hamden, Conn.: Linnet Books, 1992.

Mosel, Arlene. *Tikki, Tikki Tembo*. New York: H.D. Holt and Co., 1989.

Muten, Burleigh. *Grandmothers' Stories: Wise Woman Tales from Many Cultures*. Cambridge, Mass.: Barefoot Books, 2006.

Ragan, Kathleen, ed. *Outfoxing Fear: Folktales From Around the World*. New York: W.W. Norton, 2006.

San Souci, Robert D. *The Boy and the Ghost*. New York: Simon and Schuster Books for Young Readers, 1989.

Sawyer, Ruth. *Journey Cake, Ho!* New York: Viking, 1982.

Shepard, Aaron. *Forty Fortunes: A Tale of Iran*. New York: Clarion Books, 1999.

Sierra, Judy. *The Beautiful Butterfly: A Folktale from Spain*. New York: Clarion Books, 2000.

Steel, Flora Annie. *Tales of the Punjab: Folklore of India*. New York: Greenwich House, 1983.

Would, Nick. *The Scarab's Secret*. New York: Walker, 2006.

Yep, Laurence. *The Rainbow People*. New York: Harper & Row, 1989.

Books cited

Aardema, Verna. *Anansi Does the Impossible! An Ashanti Tale*. New York: Atheneum Books for Young Readers, 1997.

Aardema, Verna. *Anansi Finds a Fool: An Ashanti Tale*. New York: Dial Books for Young Readers, 1992.

Aardema, Verna. *Bringing the Rain to Kapiti Plain: A Nandi Tale*. New York: Dial Press, 1981.

Aardema, Verna. *Why Mosquitoes Buzz in People's Ears: A West African Tale*. New York: Dial Press, 1975.

Bruchac, Joseph. *The Boy Who Lived With the Bears and Other Iroquois Stories*. New York: HarperCollins, 1995.

Bruchac, Joseph. *Native American Animal Stories*. Golden, Colo.: Fulcrum Publishing, 1992.

Demi. *Buddha Stories*. New York: Henry Holt and Co., 1997.

Geras, Adèle. *My Grandmother's Stories: A Collection of Jewish Folk Tales*. New York: Alfred A. Knopf, 2003.

Hamilton, Virginia. *The People Could Fly: American Black Folktales*. New York: Alfred A. Knopf, 1985.

Jaffe, Nina. *Older Brother, Younger Brother: A Korean Folktale*. New York: Viking, 1995.

Jaffe, Nina. *Patakin: World Tales of Drums and Drummers*. New York: Henry Holt, 1994.

Kipling, Rudyard. *Just So Stories*. New York: HarperCollins Children's Books, 1991.

Lester, Julius. *The Tales of Uncle Remus: The Adventures of Brer Rabbit*. New York: Dial Books, 1987.

Martin, Rafe. *The Brave Little Parrot*. New York: G. P. Putnam's Sons, 1998.

Martin, Rafe. *Foolish Rabbit's Big Mistake*. New York: G.P. Putnam's Sons, 1985.

Martin, Rafe. *Mysterious Tales of Japan*. New York: G.P. Putnam's Sons, 1996.

Quigley, Lillian. *The Blind Men and the Elephant: An Old Tale From the Land of India*. New York: Scribner, 1959.

Paterson, Katherine. *The Tale of the Mandarin Ducks*. New York: Lodestar Books, 1992.

Ransome, Arthur. *The Fool of the World and the Flying Ship: A Russian Tale*. New York: Farrar, Straus and Giroux, 1990.

Stevens, Janet. *Old Bag of Bones: A Coyote Tale*. New York: Holiday House, 1996.

Yolen, Jane, ed. *Favorite Folktales from Around the World*. New York: Pantheon Books, 1986.

Image credits

Index